Where Babies Play

written by Hayley Novak
illustrated by Joey Hannaford

HARCOURT BRACE & COMPANY

Orlando   Atlanta   Austin   Boston   San Francisco   Chicago   Dallas   New York
Toronto   London

Where does this little one play?

In a pen.

Where does this little one play?

In a pond.

Where does this little one play?

In a den.

Where does this little one play?
On mother's lap!